Photovoltaic

Sarah Watkinson

First published in Great Britain in 2021 by Graft Poetry

Graft Poetry
Frizingley Hall
Frizinghall Road
Bradford BD9 4LD

www.graftpoetry.co.uk

Printed by Inprint + Design, University of Bradford

Cover image: A still from a video of nutrient transport in the mycelium of a forest floor wood decay fungus, *Serpula lacrymans*. Details from the University of Oxford Research Archive: https://ora.ox.ac.uk/objects/uuid:3fbe8c31-f695-4737-b9fd-5dcc26013462

Back cover photo: Pictorial Photography, Berwick-on-Tweed

ISBN 978-1-9998878-7-2

The title

Photovoltaic means *able to produce electricity from light.*
Life on earth is possible because green plants and plankton
convert sunlight to electricity that powers photosynthesis. All
other creatures live indirectly on this captured sunshine.

SW

Acknowledgments

For help and encouragement:
Jenny Lewis and friends at the Poet's House, Oxford;
Georgina Paul and St Hilda's College Oxford; Wytham
Woods' Conservator and researchers; The Oxford Research
Centre for the Humanities.

Romola Parish, Carrie Etter, Giles Goodla,d; Bill Jenkinson
and Oxford Stanza 2, Inge Milfull and the Back Room Poets.

Jo Bell, David Caddy, Steve Ely, Jan Fortune, Philip Gross,
Wendy Klein, Tonya Lander, Yadvinder Malhi, David
Morley, David Olsen, Lesley Saunders, Lindsay Turnbull,
Gina Wilson.

Previously published:
Poems in this book have appeared in: Antiphon, Envoi,
Finished Creatures, Litmus, Pennine Platform, Shearsman,
Spilling Cocoa over Martin Amis, Tears in the Fence,
Templar Portfolios, The Alchemy Spoon, The Interpreter's
House, The North, The Oxford Magazine, The Stare's Nest,
Under the Radar, Dung Beetles Navigate by Starlight
(Cinnamon).

Anthologies edited by Jo Bell, David Coldwell, Paul Farley,
Jan Fortune, Rebecca Gethin, Elsa Hammond, Natalie Sirrett
& Natalie Shaw, Edwin Stockdale, Joe Williams, Merryn
Williams.

Last but not least I would like to thank my publisher, Nicholas
Bielby, for his enthusiasm for this book.

Contents

For Anthony

Darwin in the Galapagos

Out in the equatorial night,
      James Island's long black foreshore is lava –
boiled-over treacle-toffee
      just set,
      still too new for life.

He sways with the deck's tilt on a Pacific swell.
      Alone in the bay
Beagle's riding-light sweeps unknown stars.
      Fitzroy has plumbed deep rifts
      between the enchanted islands – uncanny,
            each the territory of a warped creation.

What immortal hand, Darwin asks,
      framed those repellent salt-snot dragons,
      neither fish nor lizard
        – so strangely un-drownable
          and the poor cormorants,
          who hold out flightless wings to dry
            on baking barrens?

Surviving progeny of long-gone castaways –
      or God's a joker.
For proof, he shoots and packs more specimens.
      Fitzroy reads the collect of the day.

Dung Beetles Navigate by Starlight

I track my treasure home on star beams, hide
my finds in caverns, steer them clean away –
before I'm stranded in the clueless day
with all my musky gleanings dull and dried.

Straightness is all. The constellations guide
my angled legs. The facets of each eye
lock on to glimmers, sensed how? Who can say?
The system works for me. I'm satisfied.

I know those lines of light shine down for me,
the dung deposited on dewy ground,
a providence. Through moonless dark I see
in multiple dimensions, beacons round,
and every blessed night miraculously
precipitates new turds for me to find.

A Paradigm Shift in Ornithology

Birds are made of light.
The chorus is dawn.
Every morning energy crystallises
on solid objects: twigs, rooftops.

When brilliance breaks on the horizon
birds are generated at every wavelength
from quick blue tits to red cardinals
or the whole iridescence of a magpie's wing.

Their bodies are different from ours.
Caged, they may clot to solidity, but free
they don't age – you don't see old birds
perch for longer, grey at the wings, get fat.

If the morning is sunny, when each bird appears
spare energy is transformed to song
although you can't hum the tune.

At sunset they darken and vanish –
new ones will condense again at first light.

Norham Castle, Sunrise

Turner's epiphany was surely a morning like this. Too still, too bright for us, this *Fruhmorgen.*

Da stieg ein Baum. No human sound yet. All I can see, at this northern tip of England, names itself to me in an old tongue. Here, there seems no Lingua Franca word for duck which works as well as duck. This *Frühling* is no *primavera,* no *printemps*; *Ruhig* breathes its soft *g* through the rising mist of the river, which is a fast-flowing *Fluss,* not a floral *fleuve.* *Tranquillité, repos,* it's not; all bright specks and sparks, rainbows in the grass. These new-leaved bushes I can't name as *saule* – the sound speaks of sallows, sickrooms, salicylic acid; they are willows, *Weide,* and that stands for the field behind as well – *Weide*'s water meadow. It's alive with birds. *Vogel*'s made of voice and angel, the right word for the wing-borne hymns of songbirds. *Oiseau* looks elegant, but write the sound out: wuzzo?

Nesting in a flood-fixed bunch of dead grass high in the bushy bank, were flycatchers – *Fliegenfänger* – yes, that's what I saw. *Moucherolles?* – for that darting flight?

Ah, old Germanic fisherman, netting *Lachs* (not *saumon*) from the skirfare, your words still sing. Your stone shiel, long underfoot, was *Hütte*; no *chalet* could have stood these floods.

14

Ordnance Survey One-Inch Map. Sheet 90. Wensleydale

High Greenfield Pasture, Beckermonds, Far Barn
are summer fields, attractors of old trails
from hibernation fug through poached in-bye
to a curlew plateau arched between two dales
where deep-set tarns survey the flying sky.

Such joy to open wide the shippon door
then – one to drive, another hold the gate –
to loose the barging herd on to the moor
and linger on the tops with them till late.

The moor's deserted, but you're not alone.
From Ribblesdale to Yockenthwaite and Cray
fell-striding lanes host such a company
of travellers, herdsmen; future and long gone,
footlit by peat moss pools that mirror sun.

Drought at Midsummer

My daily path's all mogulled molehills, dry as terracotta.
From a high dark hole in the oak, the woodpecker nestlings
I'm listening for, give adult squawks now, overdue to fledge,
to flutter down, despite sparrow hawks; with luck, take off.

The dog, nosing deep grass, tail quivering, revels in now.
Unnamed islands breach in the shrunken river, its shallows
                                    newly transparent.
I notice chucked-in tyres. Who'd have thought
people had ditched so many? Surprising I don't mind them
                                    more –

man-made rings, like prehistoric marks on moorland rocks;
                                    relics
vortexed to the bottom, rims full of stones; uncolonized and
                                    black,
remains of whirling wheels arrested, alone in the flow –
there – and not there, as chance catspaws ruffle the glassy
                                    surface.

I'm ten again, my father's levered off a punctured tyre, made
                            good the inner tube with a patch.
Then the free-wheel tick-tick down the road and away,
to narrow lanes between wild strawberry banks.

At the bridge, the backwater's calm enough for swimming.
From February debris, dried crisp in the willows, I pull a pale
                                    stick
with enough heft to hurl as far as the deeper side. The dog
                                breasts the water,
arrows towards the splash, paddling the amber, fastens his
                            teeth on wood

turns back, and hauls out with a shake. Drought or flood, his
                                                            joy
is mine too. How we console each other, dogs and humans —
as when a Roman paterfamilias had CAVE CANEM set on
                                the doorway's marble sill
under a black mosaic hound: red collar, ears up and springing
                                                        forward.

Dog Cinquain

Walking,
we're both thinking;
you, dog; I, human thoughts.
You find a scent and follow it –
certain.

The First Green Human: The Observer Interviews Clorinda
With apologies to Elizabeth Day

Her movements are quick. I had expected a plant-like woman to be languorous, but she tells me the morning sunshine has charged her up. *I am particular about wavelength*, she says, *I am useless after midday.*

How do you dress for photosynthesis? I ask. Her lovely face is not obviously green. I wonder where she takes in the light which is her nourishment. She turns to show me. Below the halter neck of cinnamon silk her back is not tanned as I had expected, but the emerald of a chameleon on banana leaves. *I am a one-woman power-pack*, she explains, with a disarming grin. *Think of my back as a solar panel. One day everybody will be like me. It's far more efficient to convert people than to cover agricultural land in glass, or have wind turbines looming on every hill.*

So, do you eat at all? I ask, spotting an empty bowl and spoon on the rattan table at her elbow. *Bone meal and sea-salt, and the tiniest shots of rare minerals – manganese, zinc and cobalt, when I'm feeling decadent,* she admits.

She sees me noticing her diamond ring, and smiles. *He's non-green,* she confides. *And my green is not passed on. Any kids will have to work for a living.*

On leaving I turn at the gate to wave, but she is already prone again, stretched out viridian on the lawn.

Postcard from the Cat

Of their many prostheses the saddest of all are forks
to correct clawlessness. So many,
and so many different. Detachable, ranked by size,
the smallest for pinning down food −
detestable, pre-killed pap. I pity

their soft bodies propped at tables, in their paws
unresponsive metal that will never retract,
never clutch and tear with the whole arm's force,
but instead turns weakly over into a mere scoop
to push mush between their hairless lips and pointless teeth.

They never drag in a bird fully-feathered
to eviscerate, each ripping off his own piece −
but place it, plucked and too hot to lick, on a table
for the Tom to take a two-clawed 'carving fork'
and fussily dissect: first legs and wings, then breast.

And neither of these 'dinner forks' is any use
to prepare a latrine. For that
they use a 'garden fork' in a fastidious hand;
turn and pat the earth, toss plants aside,
but then, forgetting their purpose, fail to perform.

Explaining Elephants

Why can't I conjure the feel of using my nose as a snorkel, or
                                                a hose
to rinse mud from my back with a blast of water from the
                                                Ganges?

I empathise easily with most mammals. I could be a dog
and interrogate the wind with busy nostrils, waving an
                                                emoticon tail

or a horse, tearing up mouthfuls of grass and barrelling off on
                                                a drumroll of hooves.
I could even assume a hedgehog's spiked coat, or a cat's
                                elastic focus and pounce −

but not those cylindrical feet, stiff skin, monstrous stature and
                                                playful
willingness to please. Where is it from, the otherness of this
                                                huge friend

who lends us his strength to haul logs; guard temples or,
                                caparisoned for show,
allows a mahout to steer with one toe on those more-than-
                                decorative ears?

In private, they are noble; they circle their young like covered
                                                wagons,
gather to celebrate birth and death, or plan night forays into
                                banana groves.

We found the key to his shape and soul in DNA: forebears
                                        like manatees,
browsing boundless seagrass meadows, made him peaceful,
                                        with muscles

that must dream swimming. Time has grounded him. Think of
                                        him free,
afloat on the tropical swell, rolling his grey bulk in play, like a
                                        whale.

Vertical

It's still upstanding
like a warm-blooded oak tree
planted in my mirror:

curve of calf and thigh
signs on the trunk
(dot dot and down-arrow)

upper limbs each side –
and there's my face at the top
with an expression of gratified surprise –

how well it's worked,
this improbable combination – mammal, biped, female.

Seeing Hares

The morning we saw the hares
two hundred deer flowed down Glen Tilt
like a buckskin conveyor belt,
heads down, unaware
of us – as we'd been unaware

of the mountain hares
above us on dark heather – two
in winter white

and at the next turn of the path we saw
(I counted) thirty more
and every one was camouflaged for snow.

It was like meeting
in some high oratory
a vast altarpiece
known only from postcards

Seamus Heaney at the Sheldonian Theatre, Oxford

We left behind
the empty-eyed stone emperors
for an amphitheatre of moss. The god is on stage
like a swan landed on a nymphaeum,
folding his outstretched wings. He reads
of all that he has seen from his wide sky:

> truth mirrored from oceans,
> from mountain-caught pools,
> tubs and wells.

A teacher's question: *Can this be taught,*
should children learn poetry by rote?

His Irish voice:
By heart.

Yeavering Bell Means Goat Hill

Fluid as good nomads, they travel the hills.
I feel forgiven if I spot a group. They make themselves scarce
and move off, like an old friend nursing an ancient offence.

Our ways have parted since we shared these places
in a settlement of grass and milk and stones.
It's not their fault we've abandoned the hefted clans.

I come down off the summit of Windy Gyle
and stop on the col for the view. Below
and far away, are walkers, perhaps a club,
or teenagers adding a D of E medal to a CV.

Then a kid cuts a caper
and I see goats, on summer pasture.

Capricorn

All day he herds them,
bivouacs as darkness falls –
sees them in the sky.

An Asthmatic Stops to Talk to Friesian Heifers at Llanystumdwy

. . . . and then it was time to turn
back up the hill to the house,
to arrive by ten for work:
lungs tense, complain.
Half way up, cows
by a fence.
Pause.
Wait.
Want them
close. Are they used to
kindness? Ears yellow-tagged
they approach. Blow mist, confer.
The nearest swings her neck from side-to-side,
the ones behind press in. I want muzzle-touch. A rough
                                        tongue
sweeps my hand. Fellow mammal, huge bag of breath, I sync
                          my breathing with yours.

The Badger
After Michael Longley, for Chris Newman

On the table under a lamp lies the first badger
I've ever seen close-up, alive in the twilight sleep
of anaesthesia, fresh from its muddy sett,
stiff hair bedraggled, a white grin of teeth,
little upturned spade-feet earth-clogged,
in front of a hemisphere of faces
in chiaroscuro (The Anatomy Lesson)
watching Chris's measuring hands
assessing its condition, his dictated data:
'female, healthy, with undamaged teeth
not yet chipped from stones among the worms',
suggesting notes from today translated
into one of those floppy picture books
for toddlers, until he describes how her scent
of glamour lights up multiple meetings
at crossroads of their night labyrinths –
Miss Dior – and of their polyandry,
and delayed implantation so that a mother
badger sees features of numerous fathers
in her litter playing so enchantingly
in the sett's entrance, making it questionable
to me, gingerly touching the shaving-brush hair
of what is just a big underground stoat cousin,
if this free and undisturbed hill-top life
above the roar and roadkill of the Thames Valley
is enviable, especially when you're accused,
like a mediaeval leper, of spreading cattle murrain –
although falsely, according to Chris's analysis –
nevertheless, I wash my hands well before
enjoying my post-enlightenment packed lunch.

Horses as Landscape

Black in summer, shedding his winter white
Milton's not light, but rather darkness visible
Claude's the grey morning sky, and Oscar, turned red earth.

Their backs are rounded hills, moels and bells,
their manes, hedges of buckthorn and wild roses;
grazing, they move like floating islands in the field.

Their four-footed steps don't disturb the woods.
We brush beneath low summer branches,
our ears appreciating swn y dail.

Dressage Gold

Charlotte floats diagonals in the arena below
made fabulous by black heart-throb Valegro.

We – watching week-end riders – live each step,
convinced, for just a moment, that with our own

shaggy cobs and bargain ladies' hacks
(money-pits, kept at livery out of town)

we too could ride that equine learning curve
with a top trainer, learn each subtle move

to turn us mythical, hoofs thrusting ground away,
and fly from the earthbound haul of everyday.

Oxford Canal

You board at Lower Heyford;
don't quite get to Banbury.
There and back takes a whole week-end.
You won't mind, you'll soon abandon
maps, clocks and choices
for the engine's steady underwater pulse
and life between parallel lines.

You move on a lane of water
round hillsides at the pace of a horse walking;
float under roads, through the O
of a tunnel with its upside-down twin;
lift the balanced bridges, open and close locks; enjoy
the real and simple physics of it all –

and when you stop and moor, stepping out
into damp dawns, you encounter empty fields, cow-parsley
or at midnight, glow-worms in the long grass at Aynho.

Dunstan's End

'So he stepped forward into the darkness.' – Silas Marner

Gaps in the blackthorn and bryony scrub of the hedge
lead downwards to well-trodden, half-hidden paths
deeper and deeper. In the long drought of summer
I duck in out of the sun. You can wend down and down
along bumpy trails over leaf-buried spoil heaps –
it looks as if kids use it as a speedway for trail bikes
although I've never met any – until you're at the bottom
in deep mud at the pond's edge, and the dog plunges in,
stands half-submerged, and heaves out dripping black.

In winter the dark pool turns uncanny.
It rises with the rain, and seems to want you
to slip on the narrow path above and fall
helpless, past moss-hung limestone strata
to be gathered into the stonepit's oubliette.

My First Russians

The end of that summer when polio closed the lido
and Michael Airey drowned in the Crum Wheel,
my mother and I waited after school
on level meadows by a bend in the river
– a football field on winter afternoons,
but still in summer grass, still green
for – Cossacks? The sun was low,
blue shadows masked the north slope of the moor.

It was the time of danger, peace and rumour –
what if the siren changed its usual wail
for heather fires set by bottle glass
to an air-raid whoop and moan,
and what would it mean
if, one afternoon, the sky looked strange?
Strontium 90 went for new-formed bone.

They rode out then and they were like
a different species, new to me, horse-man,
man and horse a single
hurtling intention with one will, the riders
hung below the saddle at the gallop, leaping fire,
reins irrelevant as semaphore

and they were Russians. In our Yorkshire town.
I felt the ice of fear begin to thaw
as though their hoofs found grass through frozen snow.

British Mosses and Liverworts
i.m E.V.Watson

Take a magnifying glass to moss:

so many, and small enough
to be named only in Latin −

worth learning, when it's wet
and the tops are out of sight.

The cells look Escher-tiled
and only just unseen,

a dew-green skin
of water and light

rootless on rock. Between
torrents and summer drought,

moss makes the most of clouds,
spreads photovoltaics to the misted sun.

Some rainy afternoon, walk out. Look down. Enjoy
the treasure hunt: garnet on flooded slabs is *Bryum rubrum*,

bright *Philonotis* aprons a spring, and *Racomitrium*
on wind-skimmed summits, dries hoary-grey in summer, like
                                        shed wool.

In Deciduous Woods, St Brigid's Day

1

Earth-pinned, the agitated trees complain,
the ashes' crowns all thrashing twigs;
hinged at the root, rigid trunks rock
each with its own harmonic; willows
creak, rot-weakened branches fall.
The American red alder, windborne stranger
– a mainmast with dark sails of woody catkins –
sways before a gale from the North-East.

Sunlight falls weak and moonlight-cold
from cloud-veiled sky. But trees have sensed a change:
the elder's in bud, and green under its skin.
Alizarin of birch, and hazel's pallor
colour the wood's edge. Though it's arctic still
sheathed leaves of summer are set to unfold.

In Deciduous Woods, St Brigid's Day

2

The trees are listening to their nearest star
for signs that come in waves to them through space,
stronger every day after the winter solstice.
Beyond the seven shades we call a rainbow
– a blinkered vision, red to indigo –
they scan a wider spectrum for a forecast.
Red, the glint of rubies, wakes their growth –
but a gentler ray, that's dark to us, restrains

and trips their raring phytochrome to 'off' –
a far-red we can't see but plants can.
I think trees sense it at the edge of sunset,
in the last beam through a November wood
or the warning sky of a winter dawn.
It mutters to the woods: *Lie low, sleep on.*

Field Study on a Rainy Day

Any surface in the wood is world for others.
This February morning, the air
is at the dew-point, and heavy with spores
flicked, popped or exuded, according to species.

Rain smashes *gemmae* up from drop-size cups
on liverwort's green mat. Fern sperm swims to the egg
on wet leaves. *Exidia,* witch's butter, glistens
black on a log. That crust, like paint on a rock

harbours micro-pistols, water-primed to shoot spores
badged with a microscopic pattern: crescentic, segmented.
We multiply the wood's strange microbes
in Petri dishes, on pristine vegetable jelly

and watch how nature shapes them. If you're a single cell
how big is your acre? How quick to cross? By what means
                                    can you travel,
when water might hold you like treacle one minute and then
                                    vanish
into the air, leaving you stranded, incapable of growth or sex?

It's a story of relative volumes.
One can be landscape for legions.

Winter is Over
After Statius, 45-96 AD

The snow has gone; now verges green
with fore-runners of summer's tangle:
a ruffle of nettles, rosettes of celandines.

Sun lights lichened oaks, stripes the rides.
Caerulian squares, trapezoids of sky,
hang in uncurtained woods.

Alizarin alder fringes the pond's edge
where duck and drake pair
among winter's bleached reeds.

Firs bend, a breakaway gale
swirls up a scatter of rooks
like paper ashes, black on a grey sky.
Pregnant sheep wait, silent in bare fields.

June's herb-rich hay, sprung from the untied bale
cheers me, bedding of resined pine for the horse,
his warmth, wood-smoke logs and the berry-dark wine
of the Apennines, racked in my pantry.

Six Villanelles

I   A Song of Thermodynamics

Blanched cords of couch grass tangle on the fork.
Tread-moulded casts of earth mess up the floor.
Does order – or disorder – come from work?

New sunbeams pick out cobwebs in each nook.
The smallest must know what their toil is for.
Blanched cords of couch grass tangle on my fork.

What's entropy, to spiders in the murk?
For wood mice in the wainscot, what's a law?
Does their – or my – disorder come from work?

What's buried isn't dead. That's just our talk.
Worms know that our remains are what life's for
And spongy touchwood crawls upon the fork.

Earth loves decay. Its microbes feed on muck
Foul bags of bird shit, vegetable hair.
Does order or disorder come from work?

Roots live on captured sunshine in the dark.
Wake up! Smell the geosmin! Petrichor!
Fat couch grass rhizomes come up on my fork.
My order, their disorder – human work.

II.   A Song of Seasons

The trees are listening to their nearest star.
How soon the summer wavelengths – and how strong?
Nothing's as cheering as an open fire.

Log stores dwindle, piles of ash grow higher,
dry wood warms an evening, and is gone.
But trees are listening to their nearest star

prepared to raise their leaves to build from air,
green the woods and light them up with song
as Earth's tilt cheers the morning sky with fire.

Voices from children of the dinosaur
– small, in bright feathers – charm us, on the wing.
The trees drink power from their nearest star

and with green know-how, lock sun in their core.
But charms against a chainsaw? They have none.
Not much remains after an open fire.

Soon winter comes again. The days go dark.
Our walks are short, we take an axe along.
Bare-branched, the trees disclose the evening star
and nothing cheers us like an open fire.

III.   All One Breath

A body's how a genome meets the world;
the tree's an aqueduct from earth to sky.
Light sang to the shoot, and the frond unfurled.

Air's a strange country to the unborn child.
Our first-drawn breath's exhaled upon a cry;
the body, a new genome in the world.

Power swells in the plant cell, tight walled;
stems hunt the sun, the dark side giving way;
light sings the shoots up, and their fronds unfold.

Life on land is tensioned by Earth's hold;
braced and guided by her gravity,
each species fits a genome to the world.

Leaf to leaf, our crops have tiled the field
to harvest every photon from the day.
As light hits each new shoot, new layers unfold.

All that humans are, the trees foretold:
soul and mind and hand and heart and eye.
A body shows a genome to the world.
Light sings to the shoot and endless forms unfurl.

IV.   From the Genome to the Body

I'm all your plans, and all I hold is true
but on my own I might as well be dead.
There is no point in what I am but you.

I'm single, you can split me into two.
Please live and love to make me seen and fed.
I'm all your plans, and all I hold is true.

Seize the day! Metabolise, renew
my one and only code your forbears bred.
You are my point and I must live through you.

Prescribing each attractive curlicue,
I'll give you glamour, turn your lover's head,
fulfil your plans and make your dreams come true.

Let's duplicate one base pair – or a few,
widen my options – if you only would!
Today, what I'll become is up to you –

so out you go, and dance the dance, please do.
I'll tell you how to paint your feathers red!
I'm all your plans and all I hold is true.
There is no point in what I am but you.

V.   Have I Spoiled the Birds?
Gen 1: 26-28   After John Kinsella

Has my protectorate stealthily become a dominion?
Is my squirrel-baffled bird feeding station
a too casual wooing of the non-human?

Though I plant native shrubs, this isn't my garden –
 you could call my lawn 'an invasive colonisation'.
'Stewardship' of creation was our sacred trust, not
                                                    'dominion'.

My abundance of birdseed is perhaps too sudden –
disease could spread through this earthbound
                                    murmuration;
there's risk in too thoughtlessly wooing the non-human.

Beings 'alive-but-not-us', ecocriticism terms 'non-
                                            human'.
How brazen, such reductive othering of the rest of
                                            creation!
(But – might my bird feeding be a version of dominion?)

Facing the Anthropocene risks misguided intervention;
precautionary principles preclude veiling the sun's
                                            radiation.
I want every species enlisted: Eden was mostly 'non-
                                            human'.

I want the variousness of wild companions
undiminished by domestication.
Will the nuthatch still crack shells in my dominion?
At my door, the robin's glance seems all too human.

40

VI.   Tower of the Winds, March 2021

One day's wind is never like another.
Who's this, making winter in our playground?
The wind's name should foretell the weather.

Quilted coats on every child and mother!
What icy blizzard spins the vane around?
One day's weather's never like another.

Each of us treads lightly as a feather.
Collective guilt is hard to understand.
Have I, or we or they upset the weather?

'It's *Aquilo* and *Boreas* together',
we joke, and wonder: what will summer send?
– remembering warm *Auster*, bees and heather.

Dragon's breath of flarestacks fouls the ether,
venting greenhouse gases on the wind.
One year's spring is never like another;
cyclones bring new storms for us to weather.

Woodland Restoration

Among new portents – eroding stratosphere,
pandemic eruptions; our falling towers

gather up salvage,
what can be saved.

Let life rewrite itself:
atoms of words

molecules of proteins,
books of DNA

in libraries of trees.
Salvage first editions from the burning.

Garner and bank seeds,
capsules of local know-how.

Let expert jays plant acorns in the grass,
oaks spring up from flowered thickets,

new roots restore life to the scraped earth
and new branches resound with old songs.

Spring Equinox

Some day in March
the ground is firm again –

I could run down the field
to the greening wood.

Grass has pulled water
out of mud

and sent it away
into the cold wind.

Higher, the white sun
shoots blue into puddles,

outlines frost-bright leaves,
sharpens the oak bark's ravines

and lights the apse of the sky.

My Father's Bear

Your little old lead bear stands on my desk
in a space among pencils, chargers, staples and stamps
and when I try to arrange things in an orderly way

I respect his place beside a green glass paperweight
under the lamp, and feel his displeasure if I tip him over
which is easy to do as he balances upright, on small hind
                                                    paws.

Did you snatch him up
from a toy-box in your father's attic
for a talisman, when your orders came?

Home from the army, you took Bear from your pocket
placed him on the pub table like a small portable comrade
and said to my mother and me, Let's give Bear a drink

your tankard angled to the leaden lips
of the time-worn figure like a Roman household god
dug up from some once-dangerous outpost of empire.

I'd like a museum to display Bear some day
part of this British soldier's personal kit
alongside mess tin, forage cap and Sam Browne belt.

But maybe I am wrong about all this. Maybe
that business with the bear was your kindness
to a jealous little daughter you'd hardly met.

Making Sense

Salvage was the bin in the back yard
and its contents: what could be saved.
Dry leavings, nothing smelly or smashed;
a crumple of old newspaper, crackling
hide of brown paper parcels from abroad.

I listened, and looked. Mrs Savage did sewing,
and a selvedge was the edge of her cloth. Both were,
I guessed from my mother's tone, a sort of salvage;
the weave's unfrayable edge: an economical hem.
The coal tap, though? How? I waited for understanding.

Salvage, I found, was naval: wreckage classed as reusable.
I pieced together my memories with those of others.
Like bright specks in Donegal tweed, they seemed random:
my father's khaki army coat my mother dyed dark green
dripping on the line. This kind stranger she loved the best.

Salvation for me was our leaving London for moors
where the only ruins were medieval; no sign of war
but a decommissioned tank my small brother played in
at Langbar on Sunday walks to Beamsley Beacon;
new words for beauty: beck, limestone, millstone grit;

to which my school added Latin, the secret code of men.
How had Romans peppered my whole language
with their words? *'Salve!'* said the teacher. Gradually
more memories made sense. I seemed to have heard Virgil
before: **Forsan et haec olim meminisse iuvabit.*

> **Aeneid, Book I. 'One day, you will rejoice to remember
> even this.' A wartime catchphrase among army officers.*

Fire in the Forest, as depicted by Piero do Cosimo, and my mother.

The opposite of all this growing – the green
wet understorey, the heavy summer canopy –

is wildfire. A top branch struck by lightning
can set the whole trunk aflame

within its tube of bark. It roars itself hollow
like a furnace. All timber's subtle structure

is gone in one mad incandescence; white-hot,
it flushes chimaeras from the forest depths –

weird shapes tear past, running or overhead;
things we never dreamed existed, rush by.

                              *

Finally, your brush strokes dry, you thumbed
a rising smudge of chalk, white on winter trees;

and I smelt woodsmoke, saw your farmhouse
peopled. Nothing but domesticated fire

sends up that woody incense, with its sign
of human work: a chimney and a hearth.

Dieback

Fall's on its way. The days are shorter now
but the ground's still dry. I long for rain, the scent
of wet earth; for these holed and spotted leaves
to rustle underfoot, not roof me in.

I look for sky and see it through an ash
lacy with gapped foliage, the top
sunlit and lively in the wind. I love
how the long branches sway, and chase the light

up out of the horizon to stand as landmarks
at Ashbury, Ashridge, Canons Ashby – and
how its leaf-sprung wood is built shock-safe,
right for hockey sticks and hammer handles.

This warm summer, I saw the early signs
as if a fire had singed a leaf-bunch dark:
a stowaway blight has caught the trees unarmed
– *Hymenoscyphus*, loosed upon the wind

and soon the plague-felled ash will all be gone,
replaced by transient lawns. The woods move on.
Now shifting seasons baffle permanence
what new seeds will run the maze of Chance?

Barrage Balloon, Highgate 1942
i.m. Joan Day, painter

Bellied with your brush-strokes
like a weightless still-life jug,
it hangs tethered in the summer sky

above a foreground of beans trained on poles,
with those intricate red flowers I've always loved
emerging like decorations between cordate leaves.

*

I'm hanging a retrospective exhibition.
Your work grew alongside me like a sibling,
this one the first I knew: a bright kitchen garden

normal life going on; titled *Scarlet Runner*.
Husband in North Africa, me in my pram –
all was at stake, with no certain outcome;

you painted that as well: *Scarlet Runner II*,
dark opposite of the first: a ghostly figure, red cape flying,
tearing in shadows through entangling woods.

Maternity Leave in the Age of Giorgione

The Royal Academy, Room 1: Councillors
of mediaeval Venice. They'd see us
as an old peasant and her daughter, baby in a sling –
local colour for an apprentice to dot in
to an Arcadian background, after the master
has completed his immaculate Madonna,
her tender gaze and the all-knowing Infant.

No crying in the Royal Academy. We overhear
a critic, gazing at St Agatha's pannacotta breasts,
mention Tarantino; we hope to get round before
baby Lucy, teething, starts to fret again. But stop
startled by the impossible – a birth, from a tree
but not a tree. A pregnant girl – transformed!

We are imagining now
antenatal monitoring of the oak
gravid with the demi-god – Adonis
increasing in circumference,
at last the crowning, and delivery – how?
– by chainsaw midwifery?

            Saved. A shadowed cleft
opens in the bark, and some woody womb
thrusts the child-god out. Or so Sebastiano decided,
resolving a problem of this commission: to record
an ancient myth his patron, citing Ovid, believed.

We made it. At the outdoor café,
flat whites for us two, Lucy suckling,
we watch as nameless visitors go by.

Life in 4D
For Alexander

Lorenz and his dog swam the Danube, wide as a sea,
were carried three miles down to land-fall.
Ships from the Balkans churn the river today –
a swimmer might eddy into a driving wheel.
Cataracts contribute, from a catchment of Carboniferous
Alps; dolomitic; eternal, beyond circadian.

Sun-splintering peaks arose from deep circadian
workings of the ancient sun-moon sea.
Transmuted trillions of Carboniferous
plankton accreted through aeons, by slow fall
of settling spicules. Each small chalky wheel
made sea-bed limestone, raised to the wind today.

Time streams on, flowing through today.
Our clocks like watermills mark circadian
days – escapements fixed to check the wheel
as torrents whirl it round, seeking the sea,
briefly checked by dam, flume, waterfall,
through Cambrian, Permian, Carboniferous.

Geologists chart the strata; Carboniferous
beds, coal measures. Miners from today
descend to yesterday, where rich seams fall
into the mountain's heart; working circadian
shifts in tunnels, grimy-faced, far from sea
serving day by day the pithead wheel.

Might ages also circle like a wheel,
cycling new copies of the Carboniferous?
Or might time be a multidimensional sea,
speckled with islands, each one a today,
where date-lines of our world, circadian,
float free as myth – Eden, the Flood, the Fall?

The baby looks, cries, sits and stands to fall;
watches his mobile circle, spins his wheel,
mindless of parents and their circadian
life, in his sandpit edged with Carboniferous
decorative rocks. Hooray! Today
he will play on the shore of an infinite sea.

The sea will bear him if he happens to fall.
Today he laughs and spins his coloured wheel.
The cliffs are Carboniferous, life circadian.

Livia's Garden Room

'The frescoes decorated a windowless underground room . . .'

Rome's like a desert in summer,
all the interesting families gone
to their ferny villas with breezes from the hills.

Not my Augustus, though. Affairs, he says, and so we endure
the drunkards under the wall
the stink of piss and roadside crucifixions.

I could sit here all day. In my mind I walk out
across the fenced-in grass to that paradise
of pine and red fir, bay laurel, oleander

with all their fruits and flowers. Birds, perched and in flight:
finches? doves? Frescoed feathers untested
by night or weather. How would they sing, I wonder?

My underground Elysium is rimmed
by cobalt mountains, profiled but pathless. Unclear,
I complained to him, how I'd climb up for a view.

His orders, they told me: Show her nothing to fear,
no fractured peaks, no black-mouthed caves for bears.
Give Livia soft lawns for children's play.

A Young Girl Invokes Medusa in Byzantium

O Medusa, turn your Gorgon's gaze
on the men who've chased me home from the agora!

Coral-builder, goddess of the to-and-fro
of sea and stone, mineralise them!
        It's tough being twelve. In the cool dark by the tank
I wait for the music of drips to drown my hammering pulse
and my eyes recover from the city's glare,
aware again of your underwater presence.

O mortal sister, metamorphosed nymph,
weren't you also shocked once, to turn pelagic, sexual –
to find one glance aroused a swarm of boys
        and deadly jealousy? If I'd your snake-locked head

on my girl's body, I'd beam your basilisk eyes
on all of them, and leave them fossilised.

Naomi to Ruth
Ruth 1:16–17

You've fitted in perfectly.
Everybody here loves the baby.
They don't worry about you being a Moabite,
and in fact there's no need to mention gleaning,
or anything like that, at all.

Jeremiah Retires to the Sun

My land's a legacy for lizards
fields of cyclamen and asphodel
crackled to tinder
a carpet of thorns
even Mandragora can't win water
from the capillaries of clay.

Thunder lights the Troodos
and rivers rise but vanish.
Fires spring up too fast to quench,
sour the citrus wind with charcoal

but the silver-seeded cirrus doesn't care
won't yield its rain, drifts off
and the fossil aquifers lie hidden
too deep for divining.

A Cocktail

Symphytum officinale: hepatotoxic, pneumotoxic, genotoxic

Poor Emily's in hospital, she fell off a horse
and the bones are slow to mend. They had to pin
a displaced fracture of the clavicle.

It's May. A thicket of comfrey has sprung up
behind the stable, stiff with those femur stems
that signed it 'knitbone' to old herbalists.

I Google it and find the leaves are lethal
with alkaloids that save the plant from weevils
but poison every part of vertebrates.

Comfrey might well work calcium into bones
but kill you later, when the herbalist's gone.
I think I'd better take her chocolates.

Faithful Pollinator

I seem to have lost my interest in the moon.
A scent I've never met, but half-remember
rises from the forest. I meander
aimless at first, until it calls me down

through a dark of sodden bark and umber
fluttering through tangles of lianes
on waves of drunken air, antenna-drawn
to my earthbound star. I home-in and surrender:

my tongue unrolls, I feel its lengthy weight
tap a well of nectar, till I'm full
and my floral-other sets me free.

I come to myself, stow tongue and legs, take flight
cast-off from that strange vegetable pull
and rise, moon-charmed again, towards the sky.

Neonicotinoids

Out at the back they huddle
turn off, tune out, ignore
their office messages, tobacco-calmed.

Beyond the ring-road silent orchards
stare up at an empty sky.
The bees, receptors jammed,
are all on auto-reply.

The Recipe for Wolfbane
For Hilkka Helevuo

You told me about your winter journey; how, after long hours
on the main road from Helsinki, you would turn the car on to
a single track through forest, down to your ancestral place,
two miles along the lake shore at the peninsula's end. How the
headlights' bright tunnel through the dark was walled around
with curtains of lichen glowing green and white on the old
spruce trees. How this was always a home-coming, to the
mökki you named Tyttola – the daughters' house. I imagine
the stars, and the cold, and the resined air sifting through the
draped branches. The cabin is icy, quiet, woody; you light a
fire, eat and drink. You are all there for Christmas, alone and
happy in the clean air.

I am wondering if that green glow that spoke to you of home
was the chartreuse shine of wolf-bane, *Letharia vulpina*, the
reindeer lichen's toxic gold-green twin, the pair so alike in all
but colour that no-one could discover what held code for that
gold poison, sovereign against the predator slinking into the
yard, until Spribille unspooled the spell. With new primers
written in old mushroom tongues, he found the wolf-lethal
cells of a primeval yeast, shielded from diagnostic beams by
the slimy core, transcribing their old vulpinic acid recipe from
sequences invisible to conventional taxonomy.

Reasons why 'young protester will resist until death'
Escobal Silver Mine, Guatemala, 2010

Because at each season he knows where along his horizons to
     expect the sun
     and where, before dawn, the morning star;
Because he could recognise every cow – and milk her –
     blindfold
     and predict the day's weather from the wind on his
                   face;

Because his muscles remember and perform
     his family's harvests of coffee, bananas, squashes and
              peppers
     and his memory curates a map of their layout,
     according to each field's fertility
     the feel and smell of its soil, its underfoot give;
Because he still sows the maize his forebears bred from
             teosinte;

Because his whole self extends beyond his own skin
     beyond the weekday chinos and necessary straw hat
     beyond the walls of his house and its patch in the
            village
As far as the bounding profiles of his hills of silver
     their pines, oaks and cypress, their valleys, and the
           hidden path
     where his mother once picked a glittering pebble for
        him from a winter stream.

Habitat Loss

Was it lost, or never found,
the thousand-flowered tapestry
the public good, the common ground?

The bay where herring queens were crowned
the quiet sky, the fruitful sea
was it lost, or never found?

Small city squares to stroll around,
accidental, open, free
a public good, a common ground.

Translucence of a glass-dark pond
amphibian diversity
was it lost, or just not found?

A wood where chanterelles abound
that's not some shooter's property,
a public good, a common ground?

A stranger welcomed to the round
untallied generosity
was it lost, or never found
the public good, the common ground?

Rural Assets, Blenheim

Underfoot's not dirt, not soil – but earth,
skin of the planet where we live, allowed by leaves.
This morning bluebell shoots poke up. It's spring!
Moss glows green in the wood, paths run with water,
snails are on the move. Sun spotlights the palace.
Let's deny our dread at the jaundiced field,

think instead how like prairie a huge field
can feel; how a sea of barley covered the earth
last summer, foreground to a vista of the palace.
Let's pretend we're not offended at the dead leaves
of sprayed-off oat grass, forget our fear that water
flows nitrate-glutted even from the spring.

The farmer's doing his best. We spring
to his defence and praise how the field
is spread with sewage sludge, how flood water
drains off through new ditches, how gaily his earth-
moving JCB shines through quickthorn bare of leaves,
his entangled banks richer than the lawns of the palace.

The park is let for shooting; corporations fill the palace
with away-days and silver service lunches; by late spring
guides will talk of Blindheim, seen through tapestry leaves
on the eve of battle; show private rooms; Tatler, The Field
on rosewood tables; the animatronic ghost. Who on earth
eats round a rococo gold centrepiece? The ground-water

that rises at Rosamund's Well – unholy water –
sells for souvenirs, custom-bottled for the palace,
linked to a legend: King Henry and his girl, the earth
briefly theirs alone, the wildwood leaf-dark in spring
myth-haunted, concealing, with no house or field
near; horned figures, magic, eyes behind the leaves.

Then, only autumn yellowed the leaves,
lakes and streams glittered with living water.
The ploughman dreamed his fair field
full of folk who'd never see a palace –
new grass and milk made their spring,
creatures beyond imagining, their earth.

This spring walking leaves earth on my boots. My house is no
                                                          palace
but I have hot water; and my study, where I write and
                                                         field calls.

Corporate Q and A

'What does it take to be a truly effective board?'
I am proud of my straight grain, strength and resilience. Ten of us were delivered by a Stenner saw, from a felled oak dragged in chains from a southern wood.

'Discuss the importance of clearly defined roles,'
I will always feel vertical at heart, though now I am alone and horizontal. The wind no longer stretches me, I have no roots to resist it.

I am dried and abraded, waxed and polished smooth. My legs have made me immobile. The Company Directors admire my fine figuring: heartwood and sapwood, knots from branches lost to deer in my green days, even the tawny spalting from a rot that my young tissues resisted.

Spring is for their AGM, not my rush of sap. In the wood I bore acorns and suffered squirrels, now I am papered over with their accounting.

'and setting achievable goals'
In the beginning they made us for gift, communion and sacrifice. A board can host a faculty, give or withhold approval; aspire to sanctity as altar, or gravitas in its board-room.

'in our latest corporate governance article.'
I may be board now, but know this: only weather and daylength governed the wood where I grew.

Unborn, October
For Lucy

I'm picking apples without wormholes,
anticipating the moment of abscission
with a twist, piling fruit in a lamp-lit bowl.

Rain's pasted summer's dust to clay. Impressions
of horseshoes, boots, tyres and deer slots are printed
in mud, single tracks compressed to a procession.

Everything's going underground for winter,
packing away, chrysalis and armoured buds
refreshing ancestral forms. Ink caps dissolve into

sinking drops of spores; the oak's embryo waits
curating its library and dry stores. Each buried
pericarp encapsulates a new tree, canopy and roots.

Wild flowers are over, the queen bee silent in her burrow;
long nights enfold the shorter, drawing trains of days
and harvest fields. Under the heath lies the hurren,

house of your clan. Your signature name
is waiting; a variation in the key of you
composed, ready to skip out along the stave.

Wytham Woods: A Gift

'The mildest February for twenty years' – Seamus Heaney,
Glanmore Sonnets

Come in. Leave the exhausting city behind.
Walk down Marley Wood to the spring
where fresh moss green-lights the race to summer.

Pick open a winter bud of the old oaks with a thumbnail –
                                already, tiny leaves inside
are set to burst on cue, and prime a caterpillar glut
                                with captured sunshine.

Can the birds now brightening their blue crowns,
                                pecking down catkins and lichen,
still count on those soft beakfuls,
                to fuel nesting and laying, foraging and fledging?

NASA's satellite maps Wytham's temperate greening,
                                tuned to earth's annual tilt;
                a sentinel for change in the planet's vital signs.

The forest's breath is steady for now;
                the electron dance that powers the Woods' being
                                makes wood to spare.

For understanding the causes of such things
for kindly guardianship of creatures,
to brighten the minds of children
these woods were given for learning, for the love of a child.

Lockdown by the River Tweed, April 2020

'... the huge cliff
Rose up between me and the stars' – Wordsworth

No trope's as exciting as the innocent
pursued across country by an enemy.
This retreat, though, is more like a game of tag.
Touched, you're dangerous.

Between the salmon river, and the huge cliff
winter floods carved through geological time,
the path shines with celandines and violets.
But it is narrow.

We step aside on meeting, out of kindness;
researchers forecast May for the peak ahead.
A huge unstable cliff shadows our future,
the roar of rockfall.

The Tyre
After R.F. Langley

Path, steep down and sandy
river edge, bridge over,
echo under. Sandy river tilth
depths under the bridge
salmon denizen, today not seen.
White seed fluff, willow
part flood-uprooted
and re-rooted all along.
River ricochet and sediment
perennials rooting through.
Boraginaceae, soldiers and sailors
bud unroll pink to blue, waiting
a closed-wing butterfly – what?
marbled green; comfrey flower
closed. Nothing doing. Clinging-on
insect, what? Clubbed antennae.
Sensors, oddly stigma-shaped.
Stigma, flower's antenna?
Don't both sense and choose
each other? Pollinator waiting.
Nectar for pollination, deal.
Wings shiver, glint orange tips.
Open. So – not rare but stunning
one of the sixty-nine on
garlic mustard, jack-by-the-hedge.
Linnaean? And on dead nettle,
refracting metallic beetles
honey gold Chrysomelids.
And below, embedded, part-filled

sedimented débris, stuck?
Black rubber tyre. Fingers under the rim.
Light, liftable. Bounce on the grass
shake out mud cakes, heft on a shoulder,
salvage. Wildlife Kate's requirement:
DIY birdbath. Best basis for
a small pool for bathing feathers.

Sacrificial Mortar

Soft mortar lets the stones agree;
unarmoured, tolerate the rain;
lie together, each one free,
shift a little under strain.

The mortar, not the wall, erodes,
holds lightly, is the first to yield;
accommodates when ground subsides,
crumbles before stones grow old.

Such gentle bonds, put under stress
let components part intact
fit to build a better house,
disengaged but never wrecked.

Magna Carta

You say this old agreement keeps me safe,
these lines laid down by toffs on marshy ground
eight centuries back, inked by a monkish hand
on one whole sheepskin. But I wonder if

this parchment talisman can hold today –
rules for a small sea-moated patch of land,
to bind one king – how can they be maintained
now words fly into clouds and drift away?

In my street no tigers come to tea,
no secret agents watch my house at night.
I keep the law, I pay my tax, and yet
I fear, one day, more might be asked of me.

Flying Home from the Learned Conference
John 6:21

You have worked many days among strangers, speaking in auditoria with projectors that detected no signal.

The listeners have taken your handouts and vanished; they have left you alone in luxury, in a country where you do not read the language.

You shuttle away in the darkness of night; you pass unshod out of that city, before the scrutiny of the inspectors.

At the gate they enquire about your citizenship; those allowed through, hurry to board. Your seat is ready, you put away your heavy bag.

The time for departure approaches; all are accounted for, the doors closed; the pilot announces clearance for take-off.

Your plane breaks from the clouds, the wing tip sparkles among known stars; attendants smile and offer you the tea and shortbread of home.

Immediately, a sheet-bend forms in time, and a red line of dawn pulls you home. Five thousand miles pass in hours; their night becomes your noon.

In your own study, you record the words of those you heard. You find new collaborators among them; at Christmas you are glad when you receive their greetings.

A Poem about Aliphatic Hydrocarbons

Paraffins, I learned, were for beginners:
firm-strung daisy chains of atoms,
tame in their reactions, though fire
can be whipped from them by a wind.

Winter nightfall; and a blaze in the wood
at the end of our gardens was Mr Maisey
lighting a pyre of boxes; marking the end
of shop hours with a slosh of fuel and a match.

Our paraffin lived in a red jerrycan
in the shed for filtering into stoves,
a small warmth for coughing children
or to light a dim lamp in a power cut.

A lit taper to a candle – and wax
is vapour, alight in the air. Oil
flows up the wick towards oxygen:
their combustion, a silent glow.

Off Seahouses

The last thin line of land sinks below the horizon.

The boss cuts the forty-horsepower roar.
Sea-silence surrounds us.

Waves lap and splash as the RIB
(like a raft with eight survivors)
                  dips and tilts on the slow surge of the swell.

Awed, we stay quiet.
             They come
             as if from a mediaeval navigator's map
             slicing the hilly waves,
circling the marine biologist,
who back-flips into the sea
to tally them.

We peer over low rubber gunwales,
             catching their upward glances
             as they side-slip under our boat.

The scientist flops back on board
             pleased with this data point: white-
                           beaked

        a species of cool waters

Conversations at a Distance
'In Solitude, for Company' – W.H.Auden

Blue Tits
There is still warm-blooded life in these battered fields.
Among flailed twigs – a flicker of blue-sky crown, a pale
breast;
your movements like the flap and pause of a late bramble leaf
turning over in the autumn wind.

Mimicry, the protective conduct of hedge birds – presumably
perfected on former edges of wild understorey, still serves you
well.

Ring Ouzel
There is still life up here where winter hangs on
in the riever's den up in the Hen Hole, overshadowed
black peat path weaving into the hill, roar of
a deep hidden burn, scatter of old rockfall
desolation, the cold boulders we climb.
Almost unbearable, this mountain gloom. Then
over the meltwater diapason
from under a wet rock, comes your spirit song.

Curlews
understand air as an open system, adiabatic, chaotic;
how to be tossed in it, how to surf the wind's upthrust,
to swoop love songs in four-dimensional space. You two
are nothing to do with me. This demonstration
is for continuing an idea of air, beyond me,
my boots on the ground.
Although somehow
you voice my sorrow for the retreating horizons.

Hedge Sparrow
Very close to the earth, and very close
to the kitchen door, I caught you
full face, and there was no face.
Little black beak little eyes
dark as deep time.

Robin
I knew you were there all the time
when I searched the bushes with binoculars
in the green spring. Yours was the inexplicably
sad song. But now you stand plain among yellow
remaining leaves in the field-maple, singing
quite cheerfully. Perhaps to me.

Notes

p 11 In 1835 Charles Darwin accompanied Captain Fitzroy on the naval survey vessel HMS Beagle to the remote Galapagos islands, where his observations led him to the inescapable conclusion that species were not created once, as in the biblical account, but arise by an ongoing process of evolution.

P 12 Inspired by Dacke et al., (2013), 'Dung Beetles Use the Milky Way for Orientation'.

p 14 JMW Turner's visionary painting of Norham Castle, 1845. *Da stieg ein Baum ('There rose a tree')* – first line of Rilke's *Sonnets to Orpheus.*.

p 27 Moel, bell – terms for rounded hills, in Wales and Northumberland. *Swn y dail* – Welsh: the sound of the leaves.

p. 29 Charlotte Dujardin won gold in the 2012 London Olympics riding the horse Valegro.

p 30 Strontium 90: radioactive metal produced by the explosion of the warheads carried by intercontinental ballistic missiles, readily taken up by the growing bones of children.

p 36 The term *entropy* from thermodynamics is used loosely for the tendency of things towards disorder. 'Petrichor' and 'geosmin' refer to the pleasant scent of moist earth.

p 39 The genome, DNA that holds the code to build a body. Sexual reproduction, assisted by bodily characteristics like attractive feathers, passes down fresh versions of the genome.

p 40 God gives Adam *dominion* over the animals in the King James Bible. Some modern translations prefer '*stewardship*'.

74

p 42 The ancient Tower of the Winds forecast weather from wind direction: *Aquilo* and *Boreas:* northerlies, *Auster,* southerly. Climate change makes weather less predictable.

p 44 In plant transpiration, water taken up by the roots evaporatesfrom the leaves, drying the ground.

p 50 Konrad Lorenz, Nobel prize-winning ethologist from Vienna.

p 52 Livia's garden room fresco: National Museum of Rome.

p 53 Medusa, protector of women, is carved in Byzantine underground cisterns in Istanbul. 'Pelagic, sexual' – a *medusa* is the adult, sexual phase in the life cycle of the jellyfish.

p 54 'The Troodos' – main mountain range in Cyprus. Mandragora – mandrake

p 57 Inspired by Toby Spribille's discovery of previously unknown toxin-producing yeasts in some lichens.

p 58 'Teosinte' – a grass, probable wild ancestor of maize.

p 60 'The palace'– Blenheim Palace, seat of the Dukes of Marlborough, in Oxfordshire, UK.

p 62 Italicised phrases are borrowed from a document produced by the accountancy firm Grant Thornton uk.

p 64 Wytham Woods were donated to the University of Oxford by the ffennell family in 1942,

p 71 The white-beaked dolphin inhabits cold temperate to subpolar waters of the North Atlantic.